Rook **biographies**™

W9-CQO-850

Benjamin Franklin

By Wil Mara

Consultants

Nanci R. Vargus, Ed.D.
Primary Multiage Teacher
Decatur Township Schools, Indianapolis, Indiana

Katharine A. Kane, Reading Specialist
Former Language Arts Coordinator
San Diego County Office of Education

ᏆᏢ Children's Press ®
A Division of Scholastic Inc.
New York   Toronto   London   Auckland   Sydney
Mexico City   New Delhi   Hong Kong
Danbury, Connecticut

Designer: Herman Adler Design
Photo Researcher: Caroline Anderson
The photo on the cover shows Benjamin Franklin.

Library of Congress Cataloging-in-Publication Data

Mara, Wil.
  Benjamin Franklin / by Wil Mara.
    p. cm. — (Rookie biographies)
Includes index.
Summary: Briefly introduces the life of Benjamin Franklin, touching on his
inventions and his contributions to the city of Philadelphia as well as to the
newly formed United States of America.
  ISBN 0-516-22516-2 (lib. bdg.)   0-516-27341-8 (pbk.)
  1. Franklin, Benjamin, 1706-1790—Juvenile literature. 2. Statesmen—
United States—Biography—Juvenile literature. 3. Scientists—United States—
Biography—Juvenile literature. 4. Inventors—United States—Biography—
Juvenile literature. 5. Printers—United States—Biography—Juvenile literature.
[1. Franklin, Benjamin, 1706-1790. 2. Statesmen. 3. Scientists. 4. Inventors.
5. Printers.] I. Title. II. Series.
  E302.6.F8 M28 2002
  973.3'092—dc21

                                    2001008329

Do you like to do different things?

3

4

Benjamin Franklin did. He was an inventor, printer, author, and scientist. He even helped to make a new country.

Benjamin Franklin was born in Boston, Massachusetts, on January 17, 1706.

When he was a young man, he helped his brother, James, run a newspaper. He printed the pages and made sure all the words were spelled correctly.

In 1726, he moved to Philadelphia, Pennsylvania. He started his own newspaper. It was called the *Pennsylvania Gazette*.

Franklin liked to do science experiments.

His most famous experiment was very dangerous. He flew a kite during a storm. He proved that lightning is electricity.

12

In 1730, he married a woman named Deborah Read. They had two children—one boy and one girl.

Franklin was very good at inventing things. He invented the rocking chair and special eyeglasses called bifocals.

15

Franklin loved the city of Philadelphia. He helped create their first library and their first fire department. He also started a school called the University of Pennsylvania.

Franklin soon did something that was even more important.

In this time, people lived in areas called colonies, not states. The colonists were under the control of another country— England. They had to follow rules made by King George III of England. He lived all the way across the Atlantic Ocean.

Benjamin Franklin helped write
the Declaration (dek-luh-RAY-
shuhn) of Independence (in-di-
PEN-duhnss).

This important paper told England that the colonists wanted to be free to make their own rules.

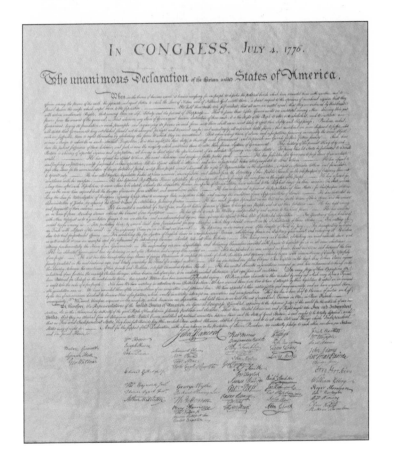

The colonists fought a war with England to win their freedom. This war was called the Revolutionary (rev-uh-LOO-shuhn-air-ee) War.

The colonists won the war in
1781. They named their new
country the United States.
Franklin helped write new laws
and rules for the United States.

These laws and rules are
written in the Constitution.

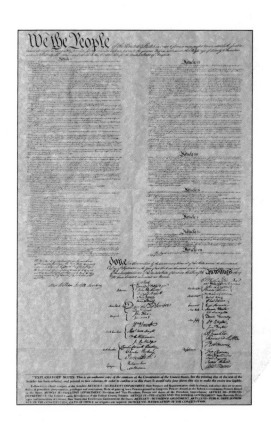

Franklin died on April 17, 1790, at the age of 84.

Benjamin Franklin made life better for other people. Many of his inventions are still part of our everyday lives.

Words You Know

bifocals

Constitution

Declaration of Independence

electricity

Benjamin Franklin

printer

Revolutionary War

University of Pennsylvania

Index

About the Author

Wil Mara has written over fifty books. His works include both fiction and nonfiction for children and adults. He lives with his wife and three daughters in northern New Jersey.

Photo Credits

Photographs © 2002: American Philosophical Society Library, Philadelphia: 12; Archive Photos/Getty Images: 7; Art Resource, NY/ National Portrait Gallery, Smithsonian Institution: cover; Bridgeman Art Library International Ltd., London/ New York/ New York Historical Society: 8, 31 top right; Corbis Images/ Bettmann: 4, 15, 16 bottom, 19, 31 top left, 30 top left, 31 bottom right; Folio, Inc./ Lloyd Wolf: 3 bottom right; FPG International/Getty Images/ Jim Cummins: 3 bottom left; Hulton Archive/Getty Images: 26 (Lambert), 22, 31 bottom left; North Wind Picture Archives: 24; Photo Researchers, NY/ Richard Hutchings: 3 top left; Stock Boston: 29 (Spencer Grant), 3 top right (Rhoda Sidney); Stock Montage, Inc.: 11, 20, 30 bottom right; Superstock, Inc.: 21, 25, 30 top right, 30 bottom left.